50 Romantic Dinner Recipes for Two

By: Kelly Johnson

Table of Contents

- Lobster Tail with Garlic Butter
- Filet Mignon with Red Wine Sauce
- Shrimp Scampi
- Pan-Seared Duck Breast with Cherry Sauce
- Grilled Salmon with Lemon-Dill Butter
- Steak au Poivre
- Risotto with Wild Mushrooms and Parmesan
- Stuffed Chicken Breast with Spinach and Ricotta
- Lobster Mac and Cheese
- Chicken Marsala
- Beef Wellington
- Pan-Seared Scallops with Herb Butter
- Grilled Lamb Chops with Mint Sauce
- Blackened Swordfish with Mango Salsa
- Creamy Garlic Parmesan Pasta
- Baked Ziti with Mozzarella and Basil
- Veal Piccata
- Grilled Tuna Steaks with Balsamic Glaze
- Chicken Alfredo with Homemade Fettuccine
- Braised Short Ribs with Mashed Potatoes
- Crab Cakes with Lemon Aioli
- Baked Salmon with Honey Mustard Glaze
- Spaghetti Carbonara
- Stuffed Bell Peppers with Ground Beef and Rice
- Caprese Salad with Balsamic Reduction
- Beef Tenderloin with Garlic Mashed Potatoes
- Pan-Seared Shrimp with Roasted Vegetables
- Veal Saltimbocca
- Miso-Glazed Black Cod
- Lobster Risotto
- Garlic Herb Roasted Chicken
- Grilled Asparagus with Parmesan
- Grilled Chicken with Pesto and Mozzarella
- Pan-Seared Duck with Orange Sauce
- Sweet Potato Gnocchi with Brown Butter and Sage

- Seared Ahi Tuna with Soy Ginger Sauce
- Herb-Crusted Rack of Lamb
- Grilled Swordfish with Lemon Butter
- Shrimp and Lobster Ravioli in Cream Sauce
- Pappardelle with Braised Lamb Ragu
- Seared Tuna Steaks with Avocado Salsa
- Roasted Vegetable Lasagna
- Pesto Shrimp and Asparagus Pasta
- Grilled Ribeye Steak with Herb Butter
- Seared Sea Bass with Lemon Capers Sauce
- Chicken and Leek Pie
- Fettuccine Alfredo with Lobster
- Spicy Tuna Tartare
- Chicken Kiev with Garlic Butter
- Seared Scallops with Lemon Butter Sauce

Lobster Tail with Garlic Butter

Ingredients

- 2 lobster tails
- 4 tbsp unsalted butter, melted
- 2 garlic cloves, minced
- 1 tbsp fresh parsley, chopped
- 1 tbsp lemon juice
- Salt and pepper to taste

Instructions

1. Preheat the oven to 375°F (190°C).
2. Using kitchen scissors, cut the top shell of the lobster tails lengthwise and gently pull apart the shell to expose the meat.
3. Place the lobster tails on a baking sheet.
4. In a small bowl, mix the melted butter, garlic, parsley, lemon juice, salt, and pepper.
5. Pour the garlic butter mixture over the lobster meat.
6. Bake for 12-15 minutes until the lobster meat is opaque and cooked through.
7. Serve with extra garlic butter for dipping.

Filet Mignon with Red Wine Sauce

Ingredients

- 2 filet mignon steaks
- 1 tbsp olive oil
- Salt and pepper to taste
- 1/2 cup red wine
- 1/2 cup beef broth
- 2 tbsp unsalted butter
- 1 tbsp shallots, finely chopped
- 2 garlic cloves, minced

Instructions

1. Heat olive oil in a skillet over medium-high heat.
2. Season the filet mignon steaks with salt and pepper.
3. Sear the steaks for 4-5 minutes per side for medium-rare, adjusting time for desired doneness.
4. Remove the steaks from the skillet and let them rest.
5. In the same skillet, sauté the shallots and garlic for 2 minutes.
6. Add the red wine and beef broth, scraping up any browned bits from the pan.
7. Reduce the sauce by half and stir in the butter until smooth.
8. Serve the steaks with the red wine sauce drizzled over the top.

Shrimp Scampi

Ingredients

- 1 lb large shrimp, peeled and deveined
- 8 oz linguine or spaghetti
- 4 tbsp unsalted butter
- 3 garlic cloves, minced
- 1/2 cup dry white wine
- 1 tbsp fresh lemon juice
- 1/4 tsp red pepper flakes (optional)
- 1/4 cup fresh parsley, chopped
- Salt and pepper to taste

Instructions

1. Cook the linguine according to the package instructions, drain, and set aside.
2. In a large skillet, melt the butter over medium heat.
3. Add the garlic and red pepper flakes, and sauté for 1 minute until fragrant.
4. Add the shrimp and cook until pink, about 3-4 minutes.
5. Stir in the white wine and lemon juice, and cook for another 2 minutes.
6. Toss the cooked linguine into the skillet and coat with the shrimp and sauce.
7. Garnish with fresh parsley and season with salt and pepper to taste.

Pan-Seared Duck Breast with Cherry Sauce

Ingredients

- 2 duck breasts
- Salt and pepper to taste
- 1/2 cup fresh cherries, pitted and halved
- 1/4 cup red wine
- 2 tbsp balsamic vinegar
- 1 tbsp honey
- 2 tbsp unsalted butter

Instructions

1. Score the skin of the duck breasts in a crisscross pattern and season with salt and pepper.
2. Heat a skillet over medium-high heat. Place the duck breasts skin-side down and cook for 6-8 minutes until the skin is crispy.
3. Flip the duck breasts and cook for an additional 3-4 minutes for medium-rare.
4. Remove the duck breasts and let them rest.
5. In the same skillet, add the cherries, red wine, balsamic vinegar, and honey.
6. Cook for 3-5 minutes until the sauce thickens.
7. Stir in the butter until the sauce is smooth.
8. Slice the duck breasts and serve with the cherry sauce.

Grilled Salmon with Lemon-Dill Butter

Ingredients

- 4 salmon fillets
- 1 tbsp olive oil
- Salt and pepper to taste
- 4 tbsp unsalted butter, softened
- 2 tbsp fresh dill, chopped
- 1 tbsp fresh lemon juice
- 1 tsp lemon zest

Instructions

1. Preheat the grill to medium-high heat.
2. Brush the salmon fillets with olive oil and season with salt and pepper.
3. Grill the salmon for 4-5 minutes per side until cooked through.
4. In a small bowl, combine the butter, dill, lemon juice, and lemon zest.
5. Serve the grilled salmon with a dollop of lemon-dill butter on top.

Steak au Poivre

Ingredients

- 2 steaks (such as ribeye or filet mignon)
- 2 tbsp cracked black peppercorns
- Salt to taste
- 2 tbsp olive oil
- 1/4 cup brandy
- 1/2 cup heavy cream
- 1 tbsp unsalted butter

Instructions

1. Press the cracked black pepper onto both sides of the steaks.
2. Heat olive oil in a skillet over medium-high heat.
3. Season the steaks with salt and sear for 4-5 minutes per side for medium-rare.
4. Remove the steaks and set aside.
5. Add the brandy to the skillet, scraping up any browned bits.
6. Stir in the heavy cream and cook for 2 minutes until the sauce thickens.
7. Add the butter and stir until smooth.
8. Serve the steaks with the creamy pepper sauce.

Risotto with Wild Mushrooms and Parmesan

Ingredients

- 1 cup Arborio rice
- 4 cups chicken or vegetable broth
- 1/2 cup dry white wine
- 2 tbsp unsalted butter
- 1/2 cup grated Parmesan cheese
- 1/2 lb wild mushrooms, sliced
- 1 small onion, chopped
- 2 garlic cloves, minced
- Salt and pepper to taste

Instructions

1. In a saucepan, heat the broth and keep it warm.
2. In a large skillet, melt 1 tbsp butter over medium heat.
3. Add the mushrooms and sauté until tender, about 5 minutes.
4. Remove the mushrooms and set them aside.
5. In the same skillet, add the remaining butter and sauté the onion and garlic for 2 minutes.
6. Add the Arborio rice and cook for 1-2 minutes until slightly toasted.
7. Add the wine and stir until absorbed.
8. Gradually add the warm broth, one ladle at a time, stirring constantly until the liquid is absorbed before adding more.
9. Once the rice is tender, stir in the Parmesan cheese and reserved mushrooms.
10. Season with salt and pepper, and serve.

Stuffed Chicken Breast with Spinach and Ricotta

Ingredients

- 4 boneless, skinless chicken breasts
- 1 cup fresh spinach, chopped
- 1/2 cup ricotta cheese
- 1/4 cup grated Parmesan cheese
- 1 garlic clove, minced
- 1/2 tsp dried oregano
- Salt and pepper to taste
- 2 tbsp olive oil

Instructions

1. Preheat the oven to 375°F (190°C).
2. In a bowl, mix the spinach, ricotta, Parmesan, garlic, oregano, salt, and pepper.
3. Cut a pocket in each chicken breast and stuff with the spinach-ricotta mixture.
4. Secure the pockets with toothpicks.
5. Heat olive oil in a skillet over medium-high heat.
6. Sear the chicken breasts on both sides for 3-4 minutes each.
7. Transfer the chicken to the oven and bake for 20-25 minutes until the chicken is fully cooked.
8. Remove the toothpicks and serve.

Lobster Mac and Cheese

Ingredients

- 1 lb elbow macaroni
- 1 lb lobster tail, cooked and chopped
- 3 tbsp unsalted butter
- 3 tbsp all-purpose flour
- 2 cups whole milk
- 1 cup heavy cream
- 1 1/2 cups sharp cheddar cheese, shredded
- 1 cup Gruyère cheese, shredded
- 1/2 tsp paprika
- Salt and pepper to taste
- 1/4 cup fresh parsley, chopped

Instructions

1. Cook the elbow macaroni according to package instructions. Drain and set aside.
2. In a large saucepan, melt the butter over medium heat.
3. Add the flour and whisk for 1-2 minutes to form a roux.
4. Gradually whisk in the milk and heavy cream, cooking until the sauce thickens.
5. Stir in the cheddar and Gruyère cheeses, paprika, salt, and pepper.
6. Add the cooked lobster meat and mix to combine.
7. Toss the cooked macaroni in the cheese sauce and transfer to a baking dish.
8. Top with additional cheese and bake at 350°F (175°C) for 15-20 minutes until bubbly and golden.
9. Garnish with parsley before serving.

Chicken Marsala

Ingredients

- 4 boneless, skinless chicken breasts
- Salt and pepper to taste
- 1/2 cup all-purpose flour
- 4 tbsp unsalted butter
- 1 tbsp olive oil
- 1/2 cup Marsala wine
- 1/2 cup chicken broth
- 1 cup mushrooms, sliced
- 1/4 cup heavy cream
- Fresh parsley, chopped

Instructions

1. Season the chicken breasts with salt and pepper, then dredge in flour, shaking off any excess.
2. In a large skillet, heat butter and olive oil over medium-high heat.
3. Brown the chicken breasts on both sides, about 5 minutes per side, and set aside.
4. In the same skillet, sauté the mushrooms until softened, about 3 minutes.
5. Add the Marsala wine, scraping up any browned bits from the pan.
6. Stir in the chicken broth and simmer for 5 minutes.
7. Return the chicken to the skillet and cook for 10 minutes until the sauce reduces.
8. Stir in the heavy cream and cook for an additional 2 minutes.
9. Garnish with fresh parsley and serve.

Beef Wellington

Ingredients

- 2 lb beef tenderloin (center cut)
- Salt and pepper to taste
- 2 tbsp olive oil
- 1/2 cup Dijon mustard
- 8 oz cremini mushrooms, finely chopped
- 2 tbsp unsalted butter
- 1/4 cup fresh thyme, chopped
- 1/2 lb puff pastry
- 1 egg (for egg wash)

Instructions

1. Preheat the oven to 400°F (200°C).
2. Season the beef tenderloin with salt and pepper, then sear it in olive oil over high heat for 2-3 minutes per side until browned.
3. Brush the beef with Dijon mustard and let it cool.
4. In a pan, melt butter and sauté the mushrooms and thyme until the mushrooms release their moisture and become dry, about 10 minutes.
5. Roll out the puff pastry and spread the mushroom mixture over the pastry.
6. Place the beef on top and wrap the pastry around it, sealing the edges.
7. Brush the pastry with egg wash and bake for 35-40 minutes, until the pastry is golden and the beef reaches your desired doneness.
8. Let the Wellington rest for 10 minutes before slicing.

Pan-Seared Scallops with Herb Butter

Ingredients

- 12 large scallops
- Salt and pepper to taste
- 2 tbsp olive oil
- 4 tbsp unsalted butter
- 2 garlic cloves, minced
- 1 tbsp fresh thyme, chopped
- 1 tbsp fresh parsley, chopped
- 1 tbsp lemon juice

Instructions

1. Pat the scallops dry with paper towels and season with salt and pepper.
2. Heat olive oil in a pan over medium-high heat.
3. Sear the scallops for 2-3 minutes on each side until golden brown. Remove from the pan and set aside.
4. In the same pan, melt the butter and sauté the garlic and thyme for 1 minute.
5. Stir in the parsley and lemon juice.
6. Return the scallops to the pan and toss them in the herb butter for 1 minute.
7. Serve immediately.

Grilled Lamb Chops with Mint Sauce

Ingredients

- 8 lamb chops
- 2 tbsp olive oil
- Salt and pepper to taste
- 1/2 cup fresh mint, chopped
- 2 tbsp sugar
- 1/4 cup white vinegar
- 1/4 cup water
- 1/2 tsp salt

Instructions

1. Preheat the grill to medium-high heat.
2. Season the lamb chops with olive oil, salt, and pepper.
3. Grill the lamb chops for 3-4 minutes per side for medium-rare, or longer to your desired doneness.
4. In a saucepan, combine mint, sugar, vinegar, water, and salt. Simmer over low heat for 5 minutes until the sauce thickens.
5. Serve the grilled lamb chops with the mint sauce drizzled over the top.

Blackened Swordfish with Mango Salsa

Ingredients

- 4 swordfish steaks
- 1 tbsp paprika
- 1 tsp cayenne pepper
- 1 tsp garlic powder
- 1 tsp onion powder
- 1/2 tsp thyme
- Salt and pepper to taste
- 1 tbsp olive oil
- 1 mango, diced
- 1/4 red onion, finely chopped
- 1 tbsp fresh cilantro, chopped
- 1 tbsp lime juice

Instructions

1. Mix the paprika, cayenne pepper, garlic powder, onion powder, thyme, salt, and pepper in a small bowl.
2. Rub the spice mixture over both sides of the swordfish steaks.
3. Heat olive oil in a skillet over medium-high heat.
4. Cook the swordfish steaks for 3-4 minutes per side until blackened and cooked through.
5. In a bowl, mix together the mango, red onion, cilantro, and lime juice.
6. Serve the swordfish with the mango salsa on top.

Creamy Garlic Parmesan Pasta

Ingredients

- 8 oz fettuccine or spaghetti
- 2 tbsp unsalted butter
- 4 garlic cloves, minced
- 1/2 cup heavy cream
- 1/2 cup grated Parmesan cheese
- 1/4 tsp ground nutmeg
- Salt and pepper to taste
- Fresh parsley, chopped

Instructions

1. Cook the pasta according to the package instructions. Drain and set aside.
2. In a skillet, melt butter over medium heat.
3. Add the garlic and cook for 1-2 minutes until fragrant.
4. Stir in the heavy cream and bring to a simmer.
5. Add the Parmesan cheese, nutmeg, salt, and pepper, stirring until the sauce thickens.
6. Toss the cooked pasta in the creamy sauce and garnish with parsley before serving.

Baked Ziti with Mozzarella and Basil

Ingredients

- 1 lb ziti pasta
- 4 cups marinara sauce
- 1 1/2 cups ricotta cheese
- 2 cups mozzarella cheese, shredded
- 1/2 cup Parmesan cheese, grated
- 2 tbsp fresh basil, chopped
- Salt and pepper to taste

Instructions

1. Preheat the oven to 375°F (190°C).
2. Cook the ziti according to package instructions and drain.
3. In a large bowl, mix the cooked pasta with marinara sauce, ricotta cheese, and half of the mozzarella.
4. Season with salt and pepper, and transfer the mixture to a baking dish.
5. Top with the remaining mozzarella and Parmesan cheeses.
6. Bake for 20-25 minutes until the cheese is melted and bubbly.
7. Garnish with fresh basil and serve.

Veal Piccata

Ingredients

- 4 veal cutlets
- Salt and pepper to taste
- 1/2 cup all-purpose flour
- 3 tbsp unsalted butter
- 2 tbsp olive oil
- 1/2 cup dry white wine
- 1/4 cup fresh lemon juice
- 1/4 cup capers, drained
- 1/4 cup fresh parsley, chopped

Instructions

1. Season the veal cutlets with salt and pepper, then dredge them in flour.
2. In a large skillet, melt butter and olive oil over medium-high heat.
3. Cook the veal cutlets for 2-3 minutes per side until golden brown and cooked through. Remove the veal from the pan and set aside.
4. In the same pan, add white wine and lemon juice, scraping up any browned bits from the bottom of the skillet.
5. Stir in capers and cook for 1-2 minutes.
6. Return the veal to the pan and spoon the sauce over the top.
7. Garnish with fresh parsley before serving.

Grilled Tuna Steaks with Balsamic Glaze

Ingredients

- 4 tuna steaks
- Salt and pepper to taste
- 2 tbsp olive oil
- 1/2 cup balsamic vinegar
- 2 tbsp honey
- 1 tbsp fresh basil, chopped

Instructions

1. Preheat the grill to medium-high heat.
2. Season the tuna steaks with salt, pepper, and olive oil.
3. Grill the tuna for 2-3 minutes per side for medium-rare, or longer if desired.
4. In a small saucepan, combine balsamic vinegar and honey. Bring to a simmer and cook until the mixture reduces by half and becomes syrupy.
5. Drizzle the balsamic glaze over the grilled tuna steaks.
6. Garnish with fresh basil and serve.

Chicken Alfredo with Homemade Fettuccine

Ingredients for Fettuccine

- 2 cups all-purpose flour
- 3 large eggs
- 1/2 tsp salt

Ingredients for Alfredo Sauce

- 1/2 cup unsalted butter
- 2 garlic cloves, minced
- 1 1/2 cups heavy cream
- 1 1/2 cups grated Parmesan cheese
- Salt and pepper to taste

Instructions for Fettuccine

1. In a large bowl, make a well in the flour and crack the eggs into the center.
2. Mix the eggs with a fork, gradually incorporating the flour. Knead the dough until smooth.
3. Roll out the dough into thin sheets and cut into fettuccine.
4. Cook the fettuccine in boiling salted water for 3-4 minutes until al dente. Drain and set aside.

Instructions for Alfredo Sauce

1. In a large pan, melt the butter over medium heat.
2. Add the minced garlic and sauté for 1 minute until fragrant.
3. Stir in the heavy cream and bring to a simmer.
4. Gradually add the Parmesan cheese, stirring until the sauce thickens.
5. Season with salt and pepper.
6. Toss the cooked fettuccine in the Alfredo sauce and serve immediately.

Braised Short Ribs with Mashed Potatoes

Ingredients for Short Ribs

- 4 bone-in short ribs
- Salt and pepper to taste
- 2 tbsp olive oil
- 1 onion, chopped
- 2 carrots, chopped
- 2 celery stalks, chopped
- 2 cups red wine
- 2 cups beef broth
- 2 sprigs fresh thyme
- 1 sprig rosemary

Ingredients for Mashed Potatoes

- 2 lbs potatoes, peeled and cubed
- 1/2 cup unsalted butter
- 1/2 cup heavy cream
- Salt and pepper to taste

Instructions for Short Ribs

1. Preheat the oven to 325°F (165°C).
2. Season the short ribs with salt and pepper.
3. In a large Dutch oven, heat olive oil over medium-high heat. Brown the short ribs on all sides, then remove and set aside.
4. Add the onion, carrots, and celery to the pot and sauté for 5 minutes until softened.
5. Pour in the red wine and beef broth, scraping up any browned bits from the pot.
6. Return the short ribs to the pot and add the thyme and rosemary.
7. Cover and braise in the oven for 2 1/2 to 3 hours until the meat is tender and falls off the bone.

Instructions for Mashed Potatoes

1. Boil the potatoes in salted water for 15-20 minutes until fork-tender.
2. Drain and return the potatoes to the pot.
3. Mash the potatoes with butter, heavy cream, salt, and pepper.
4. Serve the short ribs over the mashed potatoes.

Crab Cakes with Lemon Aioli

Ingredients for Crab Cakes

- 1 lb fresh crab meat
- 1/2 cup breadcrumbs
- 1/4 cup mayonnaise
- 1 egg
- 1 tbsp Dijon mustard
- 1 tbsp fresh parsley, chopped
- 1/4 tsp Old Bay seasoning
- Salt and pepper to taste
- 2 tbsp olive oil

Ingredients for Lemon Aioli

- 1/2 cup mayonnaise
- 1 tbsp lemon juice
- 1 garlic clove, minced
- Salt and pepper to taste

Instructions for Crab Cakes

1. In a bowl, combine the crab meat, breadcrumbs, mayonnaise, egg, mustard, parsley, Old Bay seasoning, salt, and pepper.
2. Shape the mixture into 6-8 patties.
3. Heat olive oil in a skillet over medium heat.
4. Cook the crab cakes for 3-4 minutes per side until golden brown.
5. For the aioli, combine mayonnaise, lemon juice, garlic, salt, and pepper in a small bowl.
6. Serve the crab cakes with lemon aioli on the side.

Baked Salmon with Honey Mustard Glaze

Ingredients

- 4 salmon fillets
- Salt and pepper to taste
- 2 tbsp honey
- 2 tbsp Dijon mustard
- 1 tbsp olive oil
- 1 tbsp lemon juice

Instructions

1. Preheat the oven to 375°F (190°C).
2. Season the salmon fillets with salt and pepper and place them on a baking sheet.
3. In a small bowl, mix together honey, mustard, olive oil, and lemon juice.
4. Brush the glaze over the salmon fillets.
5. Bake for 15-20 minutes until the salmon is cooked through and flakes easily with a fork.
6. Serve immediately.

Spaghetti Carbonara

Ingredients

- 8 oz spaghetti
- 4 oz pancetta or guanciale, diced
- 2 large eggs
- 1/2 cup grated Parmesan cheese
- 1/2 cup grated Pecorino Romano cheese
- Salt and pepper to taste
- Fresh parsley, chopped

Instructions

1. Cook the spaghetti according to package instructions.
2. In a large skillet, cook the pancetta over medium heat until crispy, about 5 minutes.
3. In a bowl, whisk together the eggs, Parmesan, Pecorino, salt, and pepper.
4. Drain the spaghetti, reserving 1/2 cup of pasta water.
5. Toss the pasta with the pancetta and its rendered fat, then slowly stir in the egg mixture, adding reserved pasta water as needed to create a creamy sauce.
6. Garnish with fresh parsley before serving.

Stuffed Bell Peppers with Ground Beef and Rice

Ingredients

- 4 large bell peppers
- 1 lb ground beef
- 1 onion, chopped
- 2 cloves garlic, minced
- 1 cup cooked rice
- 1 can (15 oz) diced tomatoes
- 1 tsp dried oregano
- Salt and pepper to taste
- 1 cup shredded mozzarella cheese

Instructions

1. Preheat the oven to 375°F (190°C).
2. Cut the tops off the bell peppers and remove the seeds.
3. In a skillet, cook the ground beef, onion, and garlic over medium heat until the beef is browned and cooked through.
4. Stir in the cooked rice, diced tomatoes, oregano, salt, and pepper.
5. Stuff the bell peppers with the beef mixture and place them in a baking dish.
6. Top each pepper with shredded mozzarella cheese.
7. Cover with foil and bake for 25-30 minutes, then uncover and bake for an additional 10 minutes until the cheese is melted and bubbly.
8. Serve immediately.

Caprese Salad with Balsamic Reduction

Ingredients

- 3 large ripe tomatoes, sliced
- 1 lb fresh mozzarella cheese, sliced
- 1/4 cup fresh basil leaves
- 1/4 cup balsamic vinegar
- 2 tbsp olive oil
- Salt and pepper to taste

Instructions

1. Arrange the tomato slices, mozzarella, and basil leaves on a platter, alternating layers.
2. In a small saucepan, simmer balsamic vinegar over medium heat for 5-7 minutes until it reduces and thickens.
3. Drizzle the balsamic reduction over the salad.
4. Drizzle olive oil over the top and season with salt and pepper.
5. Serve immediately.

Beef Tenderloin with Garlic Mashed Potatoes

Ingredients for Beef Tenderloin

- 4 beef tenderloin steaks
- 2 tbsp olive oil
- Salt and pepper to taste
- 2 tbsp unsalted butter
- 2 garlic cloves, crushed
- 1 sprig fresh thyme

Ingredients for Garlic Mashed Potatoes

- 2 lbs potatoes, peeled and cubed
- 4 garlic cloves, peeled
- 1/2 cup unsalted butter
- 1/2 cup heavy cream
- Salt and pepper to taste

Instructions for Beef Tenderloin

1. Preheat the oven to 400°F (200°C).
2. Season the beef tenderloin steaks with salt and pepper.
3. Heat olive oil in an ovenproof skillet over high heat. Sear the steaks for 2-3 minutes per side until browned.
4. Add butter, garlic, and thyme to the pan and transfer the skillet to the oven. Roast the steaks for 6-8 minutes for medium-rare, or longer if desired.
5. Remove from the oven, let the steaks rest for 5 minutes, then serve.

Instructions for Garlic Mashed Potatoes

1. Boil the potatoes and garlic in salted water for 15-20 minutes, until fork-tender.
2. Drain and return the potatoes to the pot.
3. Mash the potatoes with butter, heavy cream, salt, and pepper until smooth.
4. Serve alongside the beef tenderloin.

Pan-Seared Shrimp with Roasted Vegetables

Ingredients

- 1 lb large shrimp, peeled and deveined
- 2 tbsp olive oil
- Salt and pepper to taste
- 1 zucchini, sliced
- 1 red bell pepper, sliced
- 1/2 red onion, sliced
- 1 tbsp fresh parsley, chopped

Instructions

1. Preheat the oven to 400°F (200°C).
2. Toss the zucchini, bell pepper, and onion with olive oil, salt, and pepper. Roast in the oven for 15-20 minutes until tender.
3. Heat olive oil in a skillet over medium-high heat. Season the shrimp with salt and pepper and cook for 2-3 minutes per side until pink and opaque.
4. Serve the shrimp alongside the roasted vegetables, garnished with fresh parsley.

Veal Saltimbocca

Ingredients

- 4 veal cutlets
- Salt and pepper to taste
- 8 fresh sage leaves
- 4 slices prosciutto
- 2 tbsp olive oil
- 1/2 cup dry white wine
- 1/2 cup chicken broth
- 2 tbsp unsalted butter

Instructions

1. Season the veal cutlets with salt and pepper. Place a sage leaf and a slice of prosciutto on each cutlet, securing with toothpicks.
2. Heat olive oil in a skillet over medium-high heat. Cook the veal cutlets for 3-4 minutes per side until golden brown.
3. Remove the veal from the skillet and set aside. Add white wine and chicken broth to the pan, scraping up any browned bits.
4. Stir in the butter, then return the veal to the skillet and cook for 2-3 more minutes.
5. Serve the veal with the sauce.

Miso-Glazed Black Cod

Ingredients

- 4 black cod fillets
- 1/4 cup white miso paste
- 2 tbsp soy sauce
- 2 tbsp honey
- 1 tbsp rice vinegar
- 1 tsp sesame oil
- 1 tsp grated fresh ginger

Instructions

1. Preheat the oven to 400°F (200°C).
2. Mix miso paste, soy sauce, honey, rice vinegar, sesame oil, and ginger in a bowl.
3. Brush the cod fillets with the miso glaze and place them on a baking sheet.
4. Bake for 12-15 minutes, or until the fish flakes easily with a fork.
5. Serve immediately.

Lobster Risotto

Ingredients

- 1 1/2 cups Arborio rice
- 4 cups chicken or seafood broth
- 1/2 cup dry white wine
- 2 tbsp unsalted butter
- 1/2 cup grated Parmesan cheese
- 2 lobster tails, cooked and chopped
- 1/4 cup fresh parsley, chopped
- Salt and pepper to taste

Instructions

1. Heat the broth in a saucepan and keep it warm over low heat.
2. In a large skillet, melt butter over medium heat. Add the Arborio rice and cook, stirring constantly, until the rice is lightly toasted.
3. Pour in the white wine and stir until absorbed.
4. Gradually add the warm broth, one ladle at a time, stirring constantly, until the rice is tender and creamy, about 18-20 minutes.
5. Stir in the lobster, Parmesan, parsley, salt, and pepper.
6. Serve immediately.

Garlic Herb Roasted Chicken

Ingredients

- 1 whole chicken (4-5 lbs)
- 4 garlic cloves, minced
- 2 tbsp fresh rosemary, chopped
- 2 tbsp fresh thyme, chopped
- 2 tbsp olive oil
- Salt and pepper to taste

Instructions

1. Preheat the oven to 425°F (220°C).
2. In a small bowl, mix garlic, rosemary, thyme, olive oil, salt, and pepper.
3. Rub the herb mixture all over the chicken.
4. Place the chicken on a roasting pan and roast for 1 hour and 15 minutes, or until the internal temperature reaches 165°F (75°C).
5. Let the chicken rest for 10 minutes before carving.

Grilled Asparagus with Parmesan

Ingredients

- 1 lb asparagus, trimmed
- 2 tbsp olive oil
- Salt and pepper to taste
- 1/4 cup grated Parmesan cheese
- 1 tbsp fresh lemon juice

Instructions

1. Preheat the grill to medium-high heat.
2. Toss the asparagus with olive oil, salt, and pepper.
3. Grill the asparagus for 4-5 minutes, turning occasionally, until tender and slightly charred.
4. Drizzle with lemon juice and sprinkle with Parmesan cheese before serving.

Grilled Chicken with Pesto and Mozzarella

Ingredients

- 4 boneless, skinless chicken breasts
- 1/2 cup pesto sauce
- 4 oz fresh mozzarella, sliced
- Salt and pepper to taste

Instructions

1. Preheat the grill to medium-high heat.
2. Season the chicken breasts with salt and pepper.
3. Grill the chicken for 5-7 minutes per side, or until the internal temperature reaches 165°F (75°C).
4. During the last minute of grilling, top each chicken breast with a slice of mozzarella.
5. Remove from the grill and spoon pesto sauce over the chicken before serving.

Pan-Seared Duck with Orange Sauce

Ingredients

- 4 duck breasts
- Salt and pepper to taste
- 1 tbsp olive oil
- 1/2 cup fresh orange juice
- 2 tbsp honey
- 1/4 cup chicken broth
- 2 tbsp unsalted butter
- 1 tbsp fresh thyme, chopped

Instructions

1. Score the skin of the duck breasts in a crisscross pattern and season with salt and pepper.
2. Heat olive oil in a skillet over medium-high heat. Add the duck breasts, skin-side down, and cook for 5-6 minutes until the skin is crispy. Flip the duck and cook for another 3-4 minutes for medium-rare, or longer to your preferred doneness.
3. Remove the duck from the skillet and let it rest.
4. In the same skillet, add orange juice, honey, chicken broth, and thyme. Bring to a simmer and cook until the sauce thickens, about 5 minutes.
5. Stir in the butter, then pour the sauce over the duck before serving.

Sweet Potato Gnocchi with Brown Butter and Sage

Ingredients

- 2 cups cooked and mashed sweet potatoes
- 1 1/2 cups all-purpose flour
- 1 egg, beaten
- Salt to taste
- 4 tbsp unsalted butter
- 12 fresh sage leaves
- Freshly grated Parmesan cheese

Instructions

1. In a bowl, mix sweet potatoes, flour, egg, and a pinch of salt to form a dough.
2. Roll the dough into long ropes and cut into 1-inch pieces.
3. Bring a pot of salted water to a boil. Drop the gnocchi in batches into the water. Once they float to the surface, cook for an additional 2 minutes, then remove with a slotted spoon.
4. In a skillet, melt the butter over medium heat. Add the sage leaves and cook until the butter turns golden brown and the sage crisps, about 3 minutes.
5. Toss the gnocchi in the brown butter and sage, then serve with freshly grated Parmesan.

Seared Ahi Tuna with Soy Ginger Sauce

Ingredients

- 2 ahi tuna steaks
- 2 tbsp olive oil
- Salt and pepper to taste
- 1/4 cup soy sauce
- 1 tbsp rice vinegar
- 1 tsp sesame oil
- 1 tsp grated fresh ginger
- 1 tsp honey
- 1 tbsp green onions, sliced

Instructions

1. Season the tuna steaks with salt and pepper.
2. Heat olive oil in a skillet over medium-high heat. Sear the tuna for 1-2 minutes per side for rare, or longer to your preferred doneness.
3. In a small bowl, whisk together soy sauce, rice vinegar, sesame oil, ginger, and honey.
4. Serve the tuna steaks drizzled with the soy ginger sauce, and garnish with sliced green onions.

Herb-Crusted Rack of Lamb

Ingredients

- 1 rack of lamb (8 ribs)
- 2 tbsp olive oil
- Salt and pepper to taste
- 2 tbsp fresh rosemary, chopped
- 2 tbsp fresh thyme, chopped
- 3 cloves garlic, minced
- 1/4 cup Dijon mustard

Instructions

1. Preheat the oven to 400°F (200°C).
2. Rub the lamb with olive oil, salt, pepper, rosemary, thyme, and garlic.
3. Sear the lamb in a hot skillet for 2-3 minutes per side until browned.
4. Brush the lamb with Dijon mustard, then place it in the oven and roast for 20-25 minutes for medium-rare, or longer if desired.
5. Rest the lamb for 5-10 minutes before slicing between the ribs and serving.

Grilled Swordfish with Lemon Butter

Ingredients

- 4 swordfish steaks
- Salt and pepper to taste
- 2 tbsp olive oil
- 1/4 cup unsalted butter
- 2 tbsp fresh lemon juice
- 1 tbsp fresh parsley, chopped

Instructions

1. Preheat the grill to medium-high heat.
2. Season the swordfish steaks with salt, pepper, and olive oil.
3. Grill the swordfish for 3-4 minutes per side, or until cooked through.
4. In a small saucepan, melt the butter and stir in lemon juice.
5. Drizzle the lemon butter over the grilled swordfish and garnish with fresh parsley before serving.

Shrimp and Lobster Ravioli in Cream Sauce

Ingredients

- 12 shrimp and lobster ravioli
- 1/2 cup heavy cream
- 2 tbsp unsalted butter
- 2 cloves garlic, minced
- 1/4 cup grated Parmesan cheese
- Salt and pepper to taste
- Fresh parsley, chopped

Instructions

1. Cook the ravioli according to package instructions.
2. In a skillet, melt butter over medium heat. Add garlic and cook for 1 minute until fragrant.
3. Add the cream and bring to a simmer, cooking for 3-4 minutes until the sauce thickens.
4. Stir in Parmesan cheese, salt, and pepper.
5. Toss the cooked ravioli in the sauce and serve garnished with parsley.

Pappardelle with Braised Lamb Ragu

Ingredients

- 1 lb pappardelle pasta
- 2 tbsp olive oil
- 2 lbs lamb shoulder, trimmed and cut into chunks
- Salt and pepper to taste
- 1 onion, diced
- 2 carrots, diced
- 2 celery stalks, diced
- 4 cloves garlic, minced
- 1 cup red wine
- 2 cups beef broth
- 1 can (14 oz) crushed tomatoes
- 2 tbsp fresh thyme, chopped

Instructions

1. Heat olive oil in a large pot over medium-high heat. Brown the lamb chunks on all sides.
2. Remove the lamb and sauté onion, carrots, celery, and garlic in the same pot until softened, about 5 minutes.
3. Add red wine, beef broth, crushed tomatoes, and thyme. Return the lamb to the pot.
4. Cover and simmer for 2-3 hours until the lamb is tender. Shred the lamb and return it to the sauce.
5. Cook the pappardelle according to package instructions and toss with the lamb ragu. Serve immediately.

Seared Tuna Steaks with Avocado Salsa

Ingredients

- 2 tuna steaks
- Salt and pepper to taste
- 1 tbsp olive oil
- 1 ripe avocado, diced
- 1/4 cup red onion, diced
- 1 tbsp fresh cilantro, chopped
- 1 tbsp lime juice

Instructions

1. Season the tuna steaks with salt and pepper.
2. Heat olive oil in a skillet over medium-high heat. Sear the tuna steaks for 1-2 minutes per side for rare, or longer to your desired doneness.
3. In a bowl, combine avocado, red onion, cilantro, and lime juice to make the salsa.
4. Serve the tuna steaks topped with the avocado salsa.

Roasted Vegetable Lasagna

Ingredients

- 12 lasagna noodles
- 2 tbsp olive oil
- 1 zucchini, sliced
- 1 eggplant, sliced
- 1 bell pepper, diced
- 1 onion, diced
- 2 cups spinach
- 3 cups ricotta cheese
- 2 cups shredded mozzarella cheese
- 1/4 cup grated Parmesan cheese
- 2 cups marinara sauce
- 2 cloves garlic, minced
- Salt and pepper to taste

Instructions

1. Preheat the oven to 375°F (190°C).
2. Roast the vegetables: Toss zucchini, eggplant, bell pepper, and onion with olive oil, salt, and pepper. Spread them out on a baking sheet and roast for 25 minutes, stirring halfway.
3. Cook the lasagna noodles according to package instructions.
4. In a bowl, combine ricotta, spinach, garlic, and salt and pepper.
5. In a baking dish, spread a thin layer of marinara sauce. Layer lasagna noodles, roasted vegetables, ricotta mixture, mozzarella, and sauce. Repeat the layers.
6. Top with Parmesan and bake for 30-40 minutes until bubbly and golden. Let cool for 10 minutes before serving.

Pesto Shrimp and Asparagus Pasta

Ingredients

- 8 oz pasta (spaghetti, fettuccine, or your choice)
- 1 lb shrimp, peeled and deveined
- 1 bunch asparagus, trimmed and cut into 1-inch pieces
- 3 tbsp pesto sauce
- 2 tbsp olive oil
- 2 cloves garlic, minced
- Salt and pepper to taste
- 1/4 cup grated Parmesan cheese

Instructions

1. Cook the pasta according to package instructions. Drain and set aside.
2. Heat olive oil in a large skillet over medium-high heat. Add the shrimp and cook for 2-3 minutes per side until pink and cooked through. Remove shrimp from the skillet and set aside.
3. In the same skillet, add garlic and asparagus, cooking for 4-5 minutes until the asparagus is tender.
4. Add the cooked pasta, pesto sauce, and shrimp to the skillet. Toss everything to combine.
5. Serve with Parmesan cheese sprinkled on top.

Grilled Ribeye Steak with Herb Butter

Ingredients

- 2 ribeye steaks
- Salt and pepper to taste
- 2 tbsp olive oil
- 1/4 cup unsalted butter, softened
- 1 tbsp fresh parsley, chopped
- 1 tbsp fresh thyme, chopped
- 1 clove garlic, minced

Instructions

1. Preheat the grill to medium-high heat.
2. Season the steaks with salt, pepper, and olive oil.
3. Grill the steaks for 4-5 minutes per side for medium-rare, or longer to your desired doneness.
4. In a small bowl, mix butter, parsley, thyme, and garlic.
5. Once the steaks are done, let them rest for 5 minutes, then top with the herb butter before serving.

Seared Sea Bass with Lemon Capers Sauce

Ingredients

- 2 sea bass fillets
- Salt and pepper to taste
- 2 tbsp olive oil
- 1/4 cup white wine
- 2 tbsp lemon juice
- 2 tbsp capers
- 2 tbsp unsalted butter
- Fresh parsley for garnish

Instructions

1. Season the sea bass fillets with salt and pepper.
2. Heat olive oil in a skillet over medium-high heat. Add the sea bass and cook for 3-4 minutes per side until golden and cooked through. Remove the fish from the skillet and set aside.
3. In the same skillet, add white wine and lemon juice, scraping up any browned bits. Simmer for 2-3 minutes.
4. Stir in capers and butter, cooking until the butter melts.
5. Serve the sea bass with the lemon caper sauce and garnish with fresh parsley.

Chicken and Leek Pie

Ingredients

- 2 tbsp olive oil
- 1 lb chicken breast, diced
- 2 leeks, cleaned and sliced
- 2 cloves garlic, minced
- 1 cup chicken broth
- 1/2 cup heavy cream
- 1 tbsp fresh thyme, chopped
- 1/2 cup frozen peas
- 2 tbsp all-purpose flour
- Salt and pepper to taste
- 1 sheet puff pastry
- 1 egg (for egg wash)

Instructions

1. Preheat oven to 400°F (200°C).
2. Heat olive oil in a large pan over medium heat. Add chicken breast and cook until browned, then remove from the pan.
3. In the same pan, sauté leeks and garlic until softened, about 5 minutes.
4. Stir in the flour and cook for 2 minutes, then add the chicken broth and bring to a simmer. Stir in the cream, thyme, peas, and cooked chicken. Season with salt and pepper. Simmer until the sauce thickens.
5. Transfer the mixture into a pie dish. Roll out the puff pastry and place it over the pie filling. Trim the edges and brush with a beaten egg.
6. Bake for 25-30 minutes, or until the pastry is golden and puffed.

Fettuccine Alfredo with Lobster

Ingredients

- 8 oz fettuccine pasta
- 2 tbsp butter
- 2 cloves garlic, minced
- 1 cup heavy cream
- 1 cup grated Parmesan cheese
- 1/4 cup white wine
- 1 lb lobster tail, cooked and chopped
- Salt and pepper to taste
- Fresh parsley, chopped for garnish

Instructions

1. Cook the fettuccine according to package instructions. Drain and set aside.
2. In a large pan, melt butter over medium heat. Add garlic and sauté for 1-2 minutes until fragrant.
3. Add white wine and simmer for 2 minutes. Pour in the heavy cream and bring to a simmer.
4. Stir in Parmesan cheese and cook until the sauce thickens, about 3-4 minutes. Season with salt and pepper.
5. Add the lobster to the sauce and cook for 2 minutes.
6. Toss the cooked fettuccine in the sauce until well-coated. Garnish with fresh parsley before serving.

Spicy Tuna Tartare

Ingredients

- 1/2 lb sushi-grade tuna, diced
- 1 tbsp soy sauce
- 1 tbsp sesame oil
- 1 tsp sriracha sauce
- 1 tsp rice vinegar
- 1/2 avocado, diced
- 1 tbsp green onions, chopped
- 1 tbsp sesame seeds
- 1 tbsp fresh cilantro, chopped
- Salt and pepper to taste

Instructions

1. In a bowl, combine the tuna, soy sauce, sesame oil, sriracha, and rice vinegar. Mix gently to combine.
2. Add diced avocado and stir gently.
3. Season with salt and pepper to taste.
4. Garnish with green onions, sesame seeds, and cilantro. Serve chilled with crackers or on cucumber slices.

Chicken Kiev with Garlic Butter

Ingredients

- 4 chicken breasts, boneless and skinless
- 1/2 cup unsalted butter, softened
- 3 cloves garlic, minced
- 2 tbsp fresh parsley, chopped
- 1 tbsp fresh dill, chopped
- 1/4 cup breadcrumbs
- 1 egg, beaten
- 1/2 cup flour
- Salt and pepper to taste
- Vegetable oil for frying

Instructions

1. Preheat oven to 375°F (190°C).
2. In a bowl, mix softened butter, garlic, parsley, dill, salt, and pepper. Roll the butter mixture into a log, wrap in plastic wrap, and freeze for 30 minutes.
3. Slice a pocket into each chicken breast and stuff with the frozen garlic butter. Secure the opening with toothpicks.
4. Dredge the chicken in flour, dip in beaten egg, and coat in breadcrumbs.
5. Heat oil in a large skillet over medium-high heat. Fry the chicken for 3-4 minutes per side until golden brown.
6. Transfer the chicken to a baking dish and bake for 15-20 minutes, until the chicken is cooked through.

Seared Scallops with Lemon Butter Sauce

Ingredients

- 12 large sea scallops
- 2 tbsp olive oil
- Salt and pepper to taste
- 2 tbsp butter
- 1/4 cup white wine
- 1 tbsp lemon juice
- 1 tsp lemon zest
- Fresh parsley for garnish

Instructions

1. Pat the scallops dry with paper towels and season with salt and pepper.
2. Heat olive oil in a skillet over medium-high heat. Add the scallops and cook for 2-3 minutes per side until golden and caramelized. Remove from the skillet and set aside.
3. In the same skillet, melt butter over medium heat. Add white wine, lemon juice, and lemon zest, and simmer for 2-3 minutes.
4. Return the scallops to the skillet and spoon the sauce over them.
5. Garnish with fresh parsley and serve immediately.

Printed in the USA
CPSIA information can be obtained
at www.ICGtesting.com
CBHW081830191124
17645CB00018B/144

9 798330 543885